W9-CSB-186

COLOR FUN

ACKNOWLEDGEMENT

The authors, Carolyn Davis and Charlene Brown, would like to thank all of the following for their patience and support—Sally Black, Sally Marshall Corngold, Cheri LeClear, Jim Paine, John Raley and of course, the wonderful staff at Walter Foster Publishing, Inc.

INTRODUCTION

Everyone has a favorite color. With your imagination, and the use of basic color theory, color can be lots of fun. The colors we surround ourselves with show that particular colors are important to us. We use colors to describe the way we feel — for instance, have you ever heard the expression "to see red" used to describe someone who's angry? And when a friend is sad or depressed, we say they feel "blue," but when they're "in the pink," it means that they're happy again. We use different colors to describe different emotions.

Whether in decorating, clothing, graphic or fine art, you can learn how to make colors that set a certain "mood." In our study of color we will learn not only how to identify, mix and create these colors, but also how to choose and blend colors that are complementary to each other — meaning that they bring out the strength of one another (and also have a certain emotional effect for the mood that you wish to create). We'll also discover that different "mediums" (such as acrylics, watercolors, poster paints or colored pencils) make different colors, textures, and feelings — for instance, mixing blue and red watercolors makes a different color than if we mixed red and blue colored pencil.

Picking and using colors carefully is very important. Using fewer colors that are carefully chosen works best, especially if the colors are complementary to each other.

Can you imagine a color and then mix it? You are limited only by your imagination. When you let your imagination work for you, you will see that color is fun!

3.

GLOSSARY

Color—A component of sight; the sensation produced by the different effects of waves of light striking the eye.

Complementary Colors—Two colors that when placed next to each other bring out the strengths of each other. Complementary colors are exactly opposite on the color wheel. For example, red and green are complementary colors.

Harmonious Colors—Colors that go well together. Colors next to each other on the color wheel are usually considered harmonious.

Hue—The name of a color or shade of a color. Helps us to distinguish between different colors by name. Violet is a hue of purple.

Intensity—The purity or strength of a color. Mixing white, black or other colors with a certain color changes its intensity.

Mediums—Various materials used to create art. Watercolor, oil painting, pencil drawing, etc. are all mediums.

Monochromatic—Using only one color, with variations of light and dark.

Primary Colors—Red, Blue, and Yellow.

Secondary Colors—The colors made from combinations of any two primary colors. Purple, green and orange are secondary colors.

CONTENTS

MATERIALS

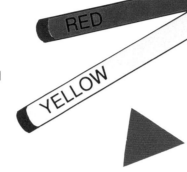

COLORED PENCILS

Pencils come in a rainbow of colors. You can buy them individually or as a set. They work best on charcoal paper, drawing paper, textured paper or illustration board.

PASTELS

Pastels are made of either chalk or oil. They come in a variety of colors and work best on a textured surface.

PAPER

Charcoal paper has texture and is good when using pastels or colored pencil. Canvas paper is perfect for acrylics and can be used like stretched artist's canvas. Illustration board comes with either a smooth surface or a soft textured surface. The soft textured surface is best for watercolor, pastels or colored pencils. The smooth surface can be used for acrylics or colored pencils. Drawing paper is good for colored pencils or pastels. All of these papers listed are available in individual sheets or in pad form.

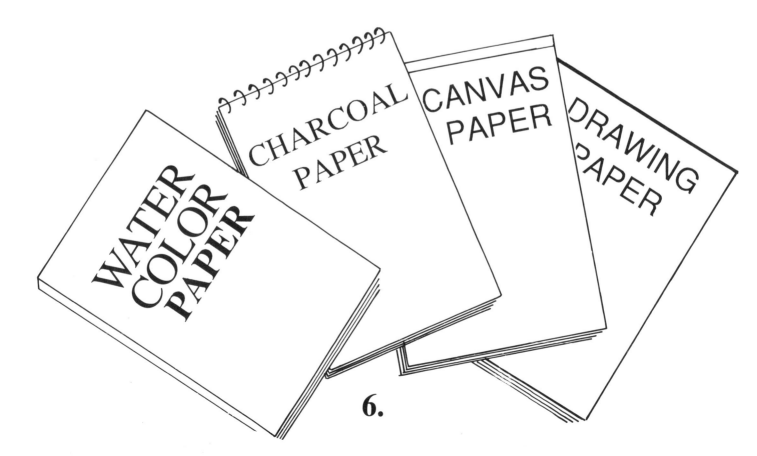

6.

MATERIALS

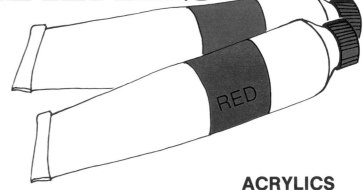

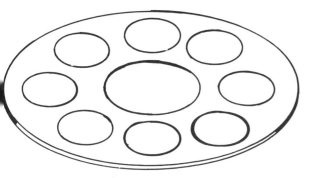

MIXING TRAY

ACRYLICS

There are many colors and a variety of brands of acrylic paint. Like oil paints in texture, acrylics are water-based and dry faster. They come in tubes and work best on canvas or heavy illustration board.

POSTER PAINT

Poster paint comes in many colors. They are opaque water-base paints and are easy to work with. They work best on illustration board or drawing paper.

WATERCOLOR PAINT

Watercolor paint comes in either a tube or a tray in a variety of colors. Watercolors are transparent and dry fast. They work best on watercolor paper or heavy illustration board.

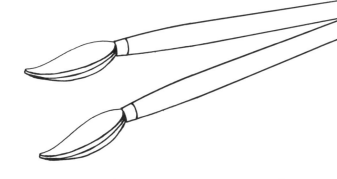

PAINT BRUSHES

There are many different sizes and bristles to choose from when selecting paint brushes. A soft sable brush is good for watercolor paint and can also be used for acrylics. A stiff bristle brush is best for acrylics.

7.

**WATERCOLOR ON
WATERCOLOR PAPER**

1.

WHAT IS COLOR?

According to Webster's dictionary, color is the property of an object that causes it to reflect light of a particular visible wavelength. But what does that mean? Color is a result of the way light bounces off of objects before that wave strikes the eye. Most objects will absorb most wavelengths of light, and reflect only one or two wavelengths (colors). The angle of the light ray as it hits an object and the molecular structure of the object itself also affect the way the color appears.

But, with or without scientific explanations, the reactions we have to color are fascinating to study—and can be lots of fun.

In this chapter we will show you primary colors and secondary colors. We will also make a color wheel, which will help us learn about the basic theory of color.

COLOR WHEEL
USING PRIMARY COLORS

A primary color is one that cannot be made by mixing other colors together. There are only three primary colors: red, yellow, and blue. They are the "parent" colors, and they are the ones you start with to make every other color imaginable.

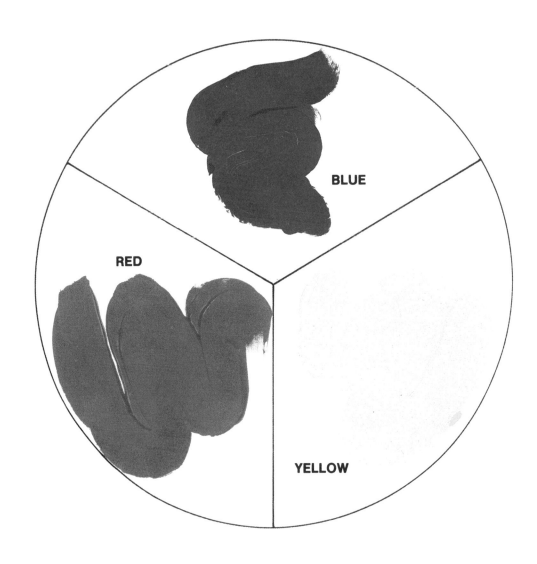

SECONDARY COLORS

Secondary colors are the colors that are made up of two primary colors mixed together in equal parts. They are placed between the primary colors on the color wheel.

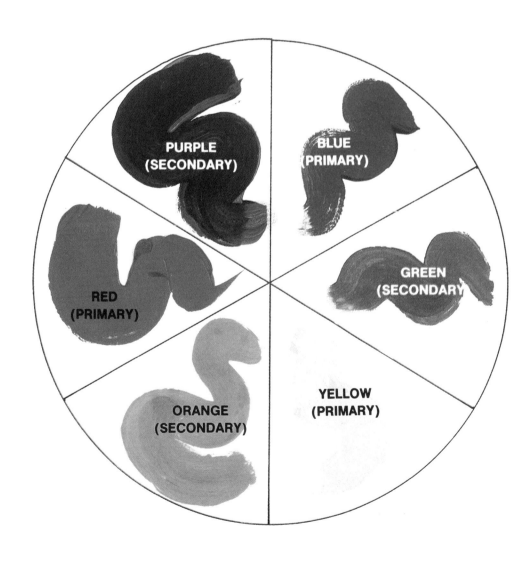

PURPLE
(SECONDARY)

BLUE
(PRIMARY)

GREEN
(SECONDARY)

RED
(PRIMARY)

ORANGE
(SECONDARY)

YELLOW
(PRIMARY)

11.

MAKE A COLOR WHEEL

Let's see how mixing the same colors, but using different mediums, can make very different hues.

1. Draw a circle.

WATERCOLOR

2. Use straight lines to divide the circle into 6 equal pie shapes.

3. Put yellow into one pie shape.

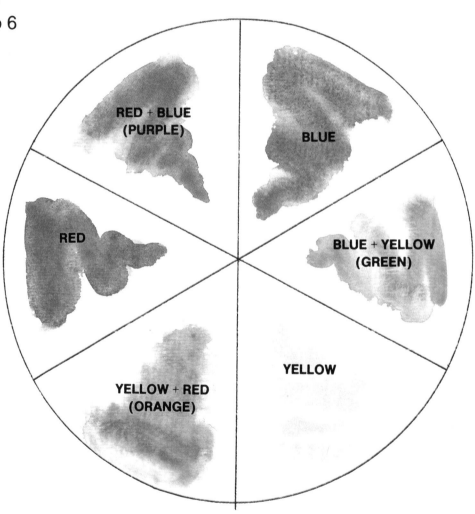

4. Skip a pie shape and put in some red.

5. Skip another pie shape and put in some blue.

6. Mix yellow and red together to make orange.

7. Mix yellow and blue to make green.

8. Mix red and blue to make purple.

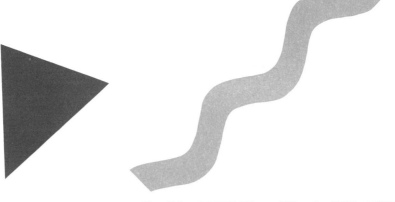

POSTER PAINT

1. Draw a circle.

2. Use straight lines to divide the circle into 6 equal pie shapes.

3. Put yellow into one pie shape.

4. Skip a pie shape and put in some red.

5. Skip another pie shape and put in some blue.

6. Mix yellow and red together to make orange.

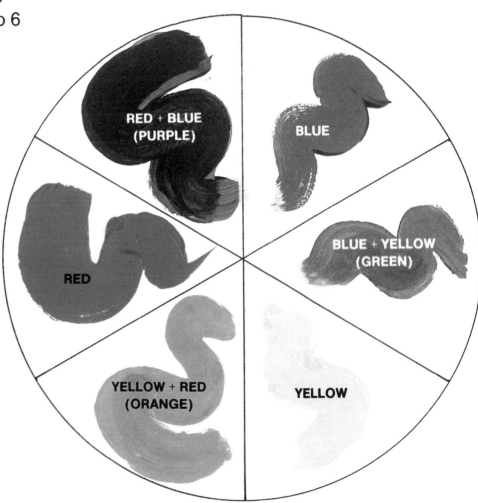

7. Mix yellow and blue to make green.

8. Mix red and blue to make purple.

13.

COLORED PENCIL

1. Draw a circle.

2. Use straight lines to divide the circle into 6 equal pie shapes.

3. Put yellow into one pie shape.

4. Skip a pie shape and put in some red.

5. Skip another pie shape and put in some blue.

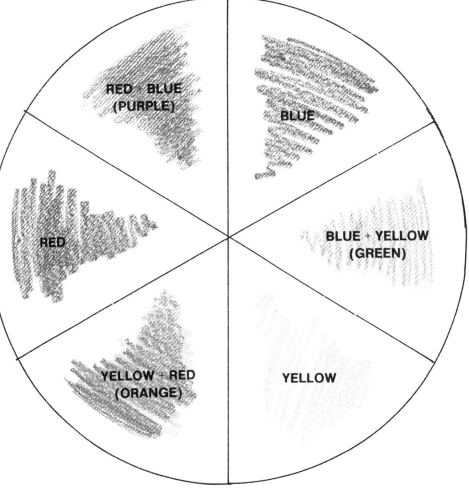

RED + BLUE (PURPLE)

BLUE

BLUE + YELLOW (GREEN)

RED

YELLOW + RED (ORANGE)

YELLOW

6. Mix yellow and red together to make orange.

7. Mix yellow and blue to make green.

8. Mix red and blue to make purple.

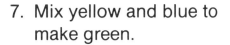

14.

MIXING COLORS IS FUN

Using the primary colors of your poster paints, make colorful finger paintings and watch how the colors mix. What a fun way to learn about color!

**POSTER PAINT ON
ILLUSTRATION BOARD**

15.

16.

WATERCOLOR ON
ILLUSTRATION BOARD

MORE COLOR

In Chapter Two we will learn how to make all the hues of the rainbow with primary and secondary colors by carefully blending from one color to the next as they appear on the color wheel. We will also learn about browns and black, which are made from all the primary colors. We will not only experiment with different colors, but also with different mediums to learn how much fun and how easy it is to mix any color we want for our picture. By trying different mediums— pastels, paints and colored pencils, we can see which ones we like best.

COLOR WHEEL
MIXING COLORS

This color wheel shows us the primary and secondary colors and some of the colors in between. The only colors we don't see here are brown and black. They are made by mixing all three primary colors together.

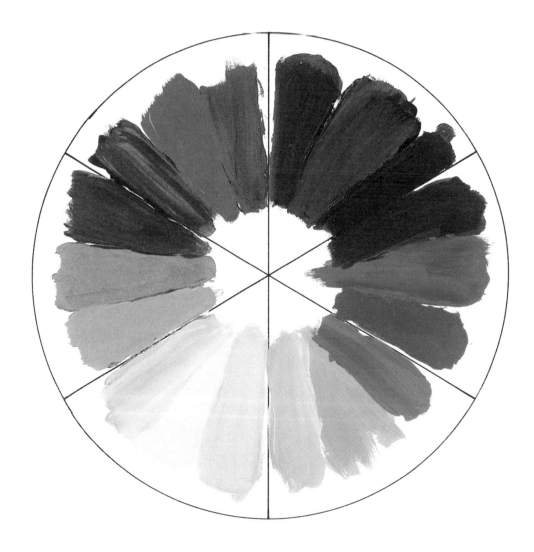

GREEN
MIX BLUE AND YELLOW

Use more yellow.

Use more blue.

Do you see the different
hues of green?

ACRYLIC

COLORED PENCILS

WATERCOLOR

PURPLE
●
MIX BLUE AND RED

Use more red.

Use more blue.

Do you see the different hues of purple?

ACRYLIC

COLORED PENCILS

WATERCOLOR

20.

ORANGE
MIX RED AND YELLOW

Use more red.

Use more yellow.

Do you see the different hues of orange?

ACRYLIC

COLORED PENCILS

WATERCOLOR

MAKE A RAINBOW

Using primary colors, make
a rainbow showing all the hues
you can.

22.

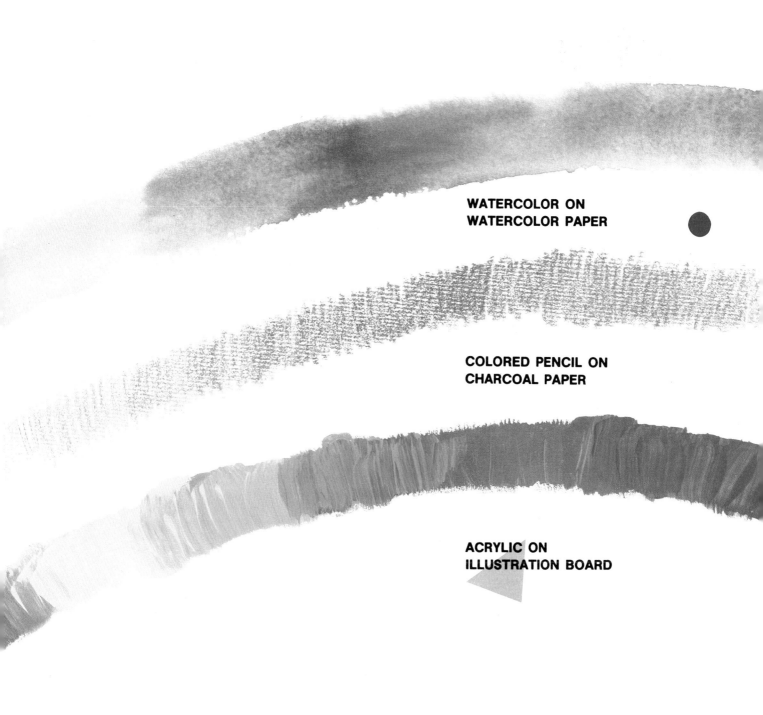

**WATERCOLOR ON
WATERCOLOR PAPER**

**COLORED PENCIL ON
CHARCOAL PAPER**

**ACRYLIC ON
ILLUSTRATION BOARD**

23.

HOLIDAY COLORS ARE FUN

GREEN

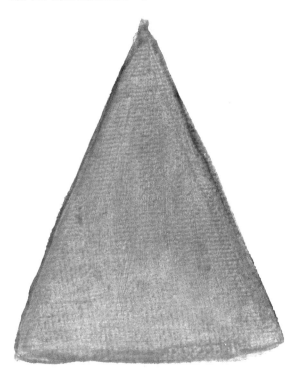

Using the primary colors, yellow and blue, to make different hues of green, you can make a bright Christmas tree.

Add more yellow to make the stem of a pumpkin.

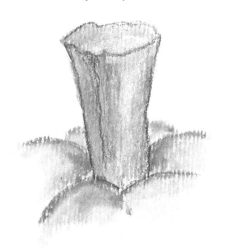

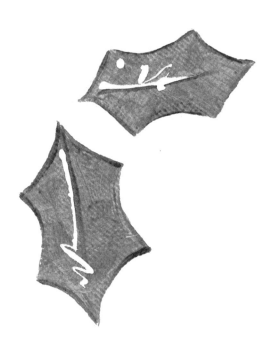

Or more blue for holly leaves.

24.

PURPLE

Mix blue and red together to make different hues of purple for an Easter basket full of eggs.

Add more red to make a rich hue of purple for Christmas decorations.

25.

ORANGE

Mix red and yellow together for different hues of orange to make a jack-o-lantern.

Add more yellow for the bright candle inside of your jack-o-lantern.

Add more red to make holly berries.

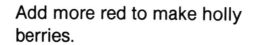

Now you can make holiday cards with bright, festive colors.

27.

**WATERCOLOR ON
ILLUSTRATION BOARD**

28.

PURE COLORS

When artists talk about the "purity" of a color, they mean that the color does not have other colors blended with it — which may gray the color. To change the intensity of the color (which is simply changing the strength or brightness of it), you add white. The purpose of changing the intensity of a color is to add texture or shape to your painting or picture to make it more realistic. Add white to blue to make a sky blue, paint different intensities of blue in your sky to make a billowy soft, cloudy sky. If we add white to red, we get a bright pink; more white and we get a baby pink. Learning to work with the intensity of color adds more dimension to our color painting or picture. We will use different mediums to experiment with as we learn about changing the intensity of colors. With some mediums, like watercolor, we can't add white, so we just add more water.

See which you like the best, and remember — **have fun!**

ADD WHITE

Change the intensity of your color
by adding white. Try acrylic paint
on illustration board.

LESS INTENSE   **TO**   **MORE INTENSE**

Change the intensity of your color
by adding white. Pastels on
charcoal paper.

LESS INTENSE   **TO**   **MORE INTENSE**

USE LESS COLOR

When using watercolor, add more water
and less color to change the intensity.
Watercolor on watercolor paper.

LESS INTENSE   **TO**   **MORE INTENSE**

When using colored pensils, add less color to change the intensity. Colored pencil on charcoal paper.

LESS INTENSE   **TO**   **MORE INTENSE**

33.

USE PURE COLORS

How to use intensity of color in your pictures.

BLUE SKY

Watercolor: when you add
more water and less color,
you can make the clouds look
billowy.

GREEN HILLSIDE

Poster paints: when you add
white paint to green, you can
make the hillside slope.

YELLOW SUN

Pastels: add white to the sun and round it out.

**COLORED PENCILS ON
CHARCOAL PAPER**

ORANGE, RED, PURPLE TULIP

35.

Shading darker and lighter gives lifelike shape to the tulip.

PASTELS ON
CHARCOAL PAPER

36.

4.

DARK AND LIGHT

The value of a color is somewhat like the intensity, but there are some differences. Add black and the result is a "shading." Add gray and the result is a "tone" of the original color—and if we add white, we get a "tint." For example, pink is a tint made of red with white added, and burgundy is a shade of red with black added. This works for all colors.

By using different values of a color you can do a complete drawing in one color. This kind of drawing is called "monochromic," which is from the Greek language and means "of one color." You can have a lot of fun with just one color. You can also add dimension to your color drawing by shading with black or tinting with white.

Come see how much fun one color can be!

BLACK

Black can be important and can be used to change the value of our colors.

Black is made by mixing all three primary colors together in equal parts.

Try mixing black.

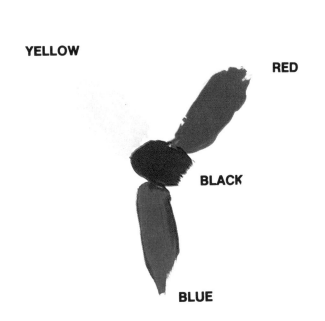

YELLOW

RED

BLACK

BLUE

ACRYLIC

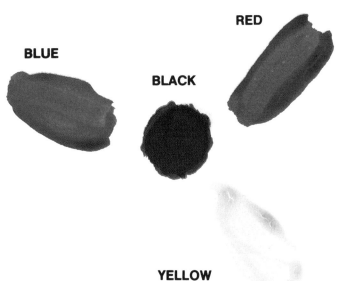

BLUE

RED

BLACK

YELLOW

POSTER PAINT

BROWN

Brown is often needed to complete a drawing.

Try mixing brown.

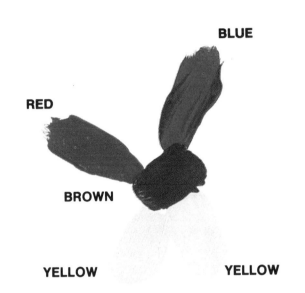

BLUE

RED

BROWN

YELLOW   **YELLOW**

ACRYLIC

PASTELS
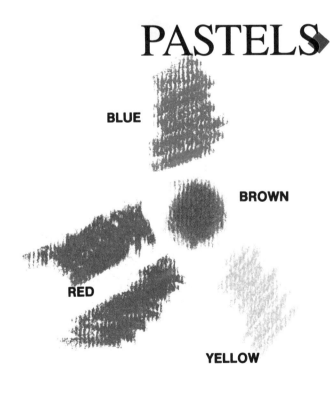

BLUE

BROWN

RED

YELLOW

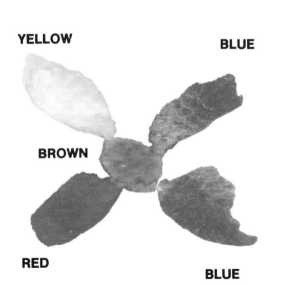

YELLOW   **BLUE**

BROWN

RED   **BLUE**

WATERCOLOR

39.

CHANGING VALUES

Change the value of your color: add white to make a lighter value or black to make a darker value.

PASTELS

WHITE   **BLACK**

GREEN

BLUE

PURPLE

RED

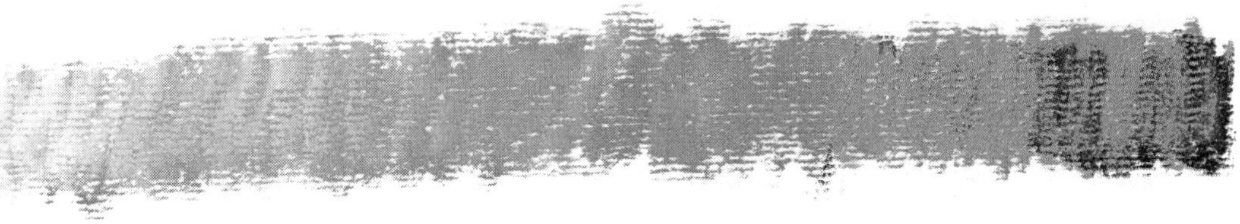

ORANGE

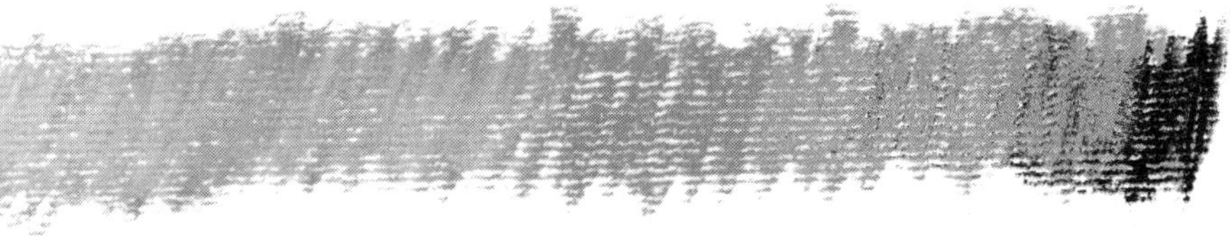

YELLOW

ACRYLIC

GREEN

BLUE

PURPLE

RED

ORANGE

YELLOW

WATERCOLOR

GREEN

BLUE

PURPLE

RED

ORANGE

YELLOW

COLORED PENCILS

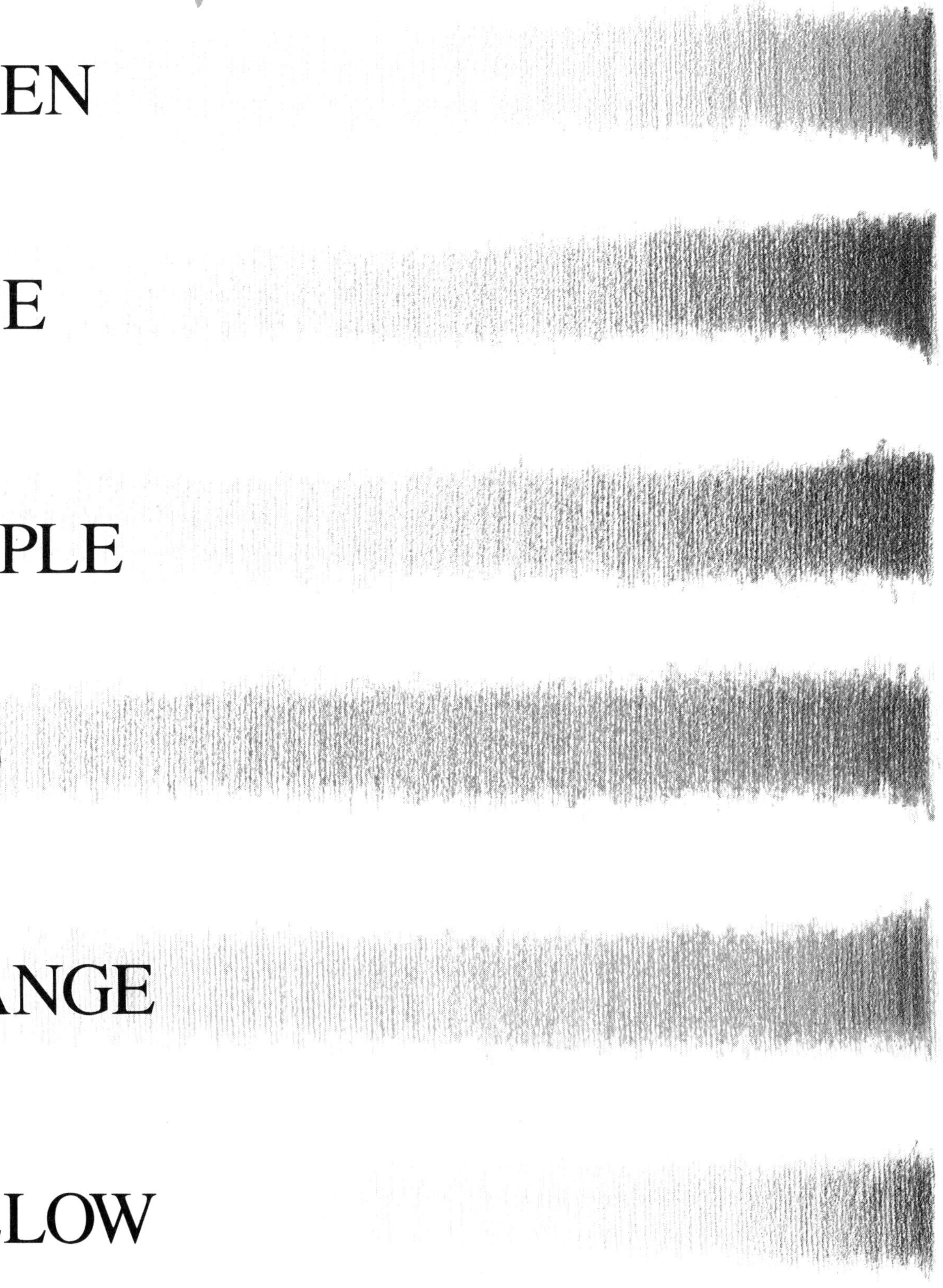

GREEN

BLUE

PURPLE

RED

ORANGE

YELLOW

43.

USE COLOR VALUES TO SHADE

BLUE

A monochromatic unicorn
in blue colored pencil.

**COLORED PENCIL
ON CHARCOAL PAPER**

44.

RED

Red balloons in poster paints on illustration board.

45.

YELLOW
A striped kitty in
yellow pastels.

46.

GREEN

A dinosaur walking through
the trees in shades of green
watercolors.

47.

ORANGE

A pumpkin on a fence in values of orange.

ACRYLIC ON CANVAS PAPER

48.

PURPLE

A magic dragon in watercolor on illustration board

49.

ACRYLIC ON CANVAS PAPER

50

5.

COLOR SCHEMES

Learn to pick your colors carefully.

Colors create moods. Some colors are warm and cheery, others are soft and soothing. Colors can be put together in special ways to give your picture a mood. Experimenting with color combinations is the best way of learning how to create the mood you want. Sometimes the color combinations won't look right or will make other colors around it look different. Color will sometimes look better with other colors. By knowing some basic rules you can better select colors.

Knowing more about color makes it a lot more fun.

COMPLEMENTARY COLORS

You can find complementary colors by using your color wheel.

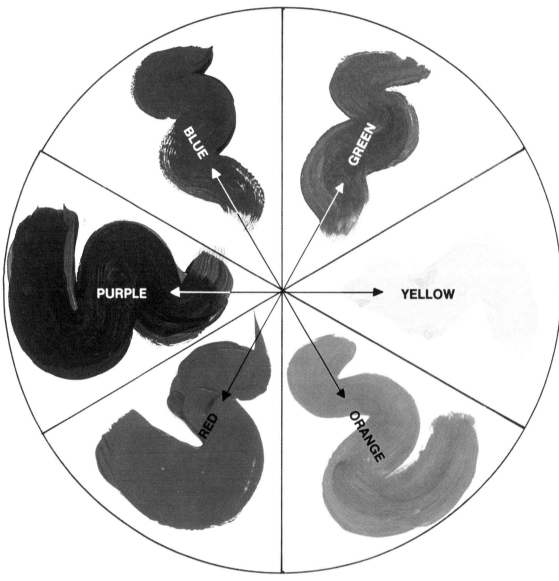

BLUE

GREEN

PURPLE

YELLOW

RED

ORANGE

Complementary colors are any two colors directly across from each other on the color wheel.

EXAMPLE:

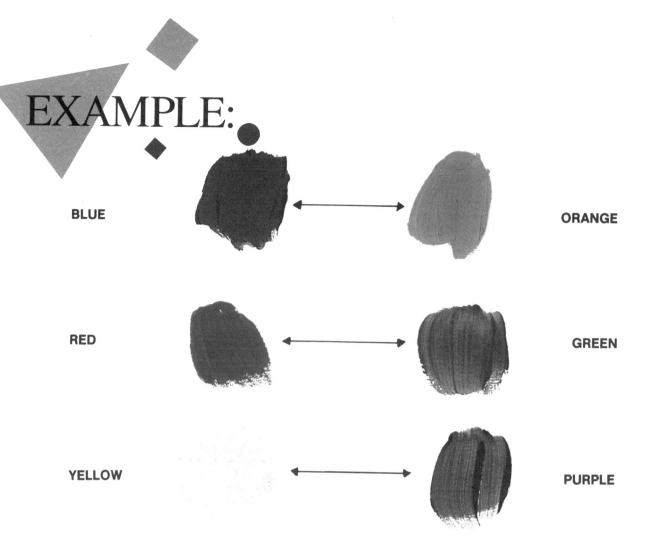

BLUE ←→ ORANGE

RED ←→ GREEN

YELLOW ←→ PURPLE

Mix two complementary
colors and you have made a
shade of brown.

RED   GREEN

YELLOW   PURPLE

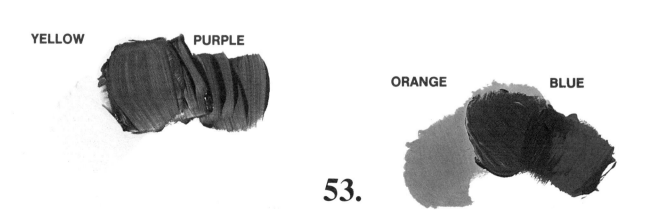

ORANGE   BLUE

53.

COLOR MOODS
BRIGHT AND CHEERY

Half of your color wheel is the bright side, and the colors found there are usually considered to be happy, warm, bold, fun colors.

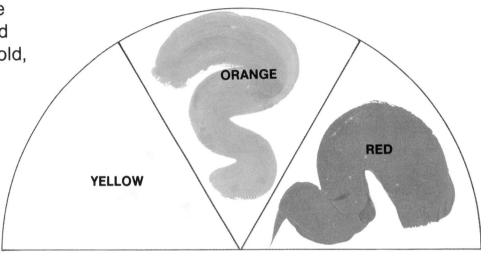

YELLOW

ORANGE

RED

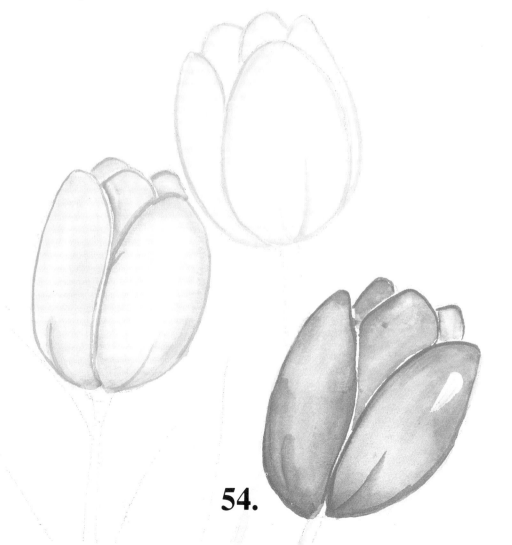

54.

SOFT AND SOOTHING

The other half of the color wheel is made up of soft, soothing, cool, sad, relaxed, passive, moody colors.

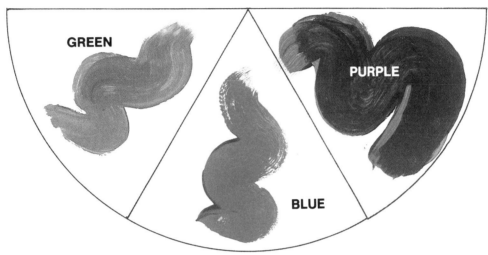

55.

COMPLEMENTARY COLORS YELLOW AND PURPLE

Complementary purple and
yellow colored pencils give bunny
a soft, spring look.

ORANGE AND BLUE

These butterflies look playful in hues of orange and blue watercolor.

Use poster paint in red and green complementary colors to paint a parrot.

58.

COLOR MOODS

A clown is brighter and more cheerful in warm colors of acrylic paint chosen from the color wheel.

LOUD BLUE–RED–YELLOW

These party favors are fun, bright, pure pastels.

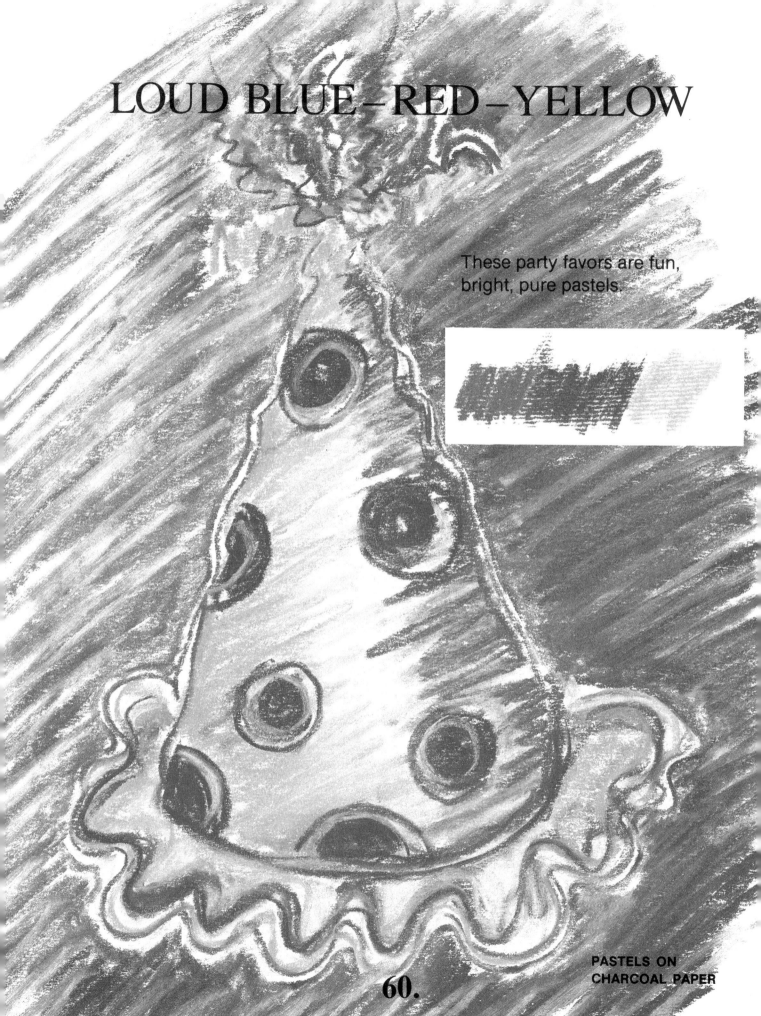

PASTELS ON CHARCOAL PAPER

**WATERCOLOR ON
WATERCOLOR PAPER**

SOFT BLUES,
PURPLE AND GREEN

The fish look cool and quiet in
watercolor paints from the cool
side of the color wheel.

PRIMARY COLORS ON BLACK.

Fireworks in the night feel fun and gay. Use bright acrylics on black illustration board.